BUILDING A BETTER BOARD
BOOK I

BUILDING A BETTER BOARD
BOOK I
BOOK I
A Guide To Effective Leadership

ANDREW SWANSON

FUND RAISING INSTITUTE
A Division of The Taft Group
Rockville, Maryland

Published by
Fund Raising Institute
A Division of the Taft Group
12300 Twinbrook Parkway, Suite 520
Rockville, MD 20852

Printed in the United States of America

96   95   94   93   92   91   6   5   4   3   2

Library of Congress Catalog Card Number: 91-73910
ISBN 0-930807-28-6

Fund Raising Institute publishes books on fund raising, philanthropy, and
nonprofit management. To request sales information, or a copy of our catalog,
please write us at the above address or call 1-800-877-TAFT.

For Shirley

Contents

Preface

It has been seven years since the first edition of this book was published by the Taft Group. Our original and continuing objective was and is to offer board members a concise guide to the basics of being an effective member of a nonprofit board. Over those intervening years the literature on boards has grown, accompanied by an increasing awareness of the importance of boards to the organizations they serve. During this period I have had the privilege and pleasure of continuing my work with hundreds of additional boards either singly or in groups at conferences and have continued to learn from all of these experiences. Houle (1989) put it well when he said ". . . it is a happy and fortunate fact about boards that the lessons that experience teaches about them are inexhaustible." My thinking about boards has naturally evolved somewhat due to these experiences and the time has come to incorporate into this book the lessons of the past seven years. I am also adding a companion volume to this book, *Building a Better Board, Book II: The Role of the Nonprofit Board in Strategic Planning*, which will deal with the nonprofit board's role in strategic planning.

Introduction

Welcome to the Board

Whether you are new to your board of directors or one of the older hands you undoubtedly know that, in accepting a seat on this board, you are taking on an important responsibility—important not only to your community, but very important to the constituency or clientele your organization serves.

Over the years it has been my good fortune to have been able to serve on, as well as to have observed, trained, and consulted with, a large number of boards in a wide variety of fields. From this experience I have learned that the effectiveness of board members and the degree of satisfaction that they derive from their effort is in direct proportion to their understanding of how effective boards work and their ability to build proper relationships among the board of directors, the CEO, and the staff, who carry out the mission of the organization.

In this book I want to share with you many of the techniques used by effective boards, and to help you become the best board member you can be.

How This Book Will Help You Become a Better Board Member

As a result of reading this book you will:

- Gain a better understanding of the role and responsibilities of your board as a whole.

- Learn what is expected of you as an individual member of your board.

- Understand your board's relationship to the CEO and to the staff as well as your individual relationship to the CEO and to the staff.

- Learn to apply the principles of plan-based governance as well as about the concomitant need for your board of directors to establish mission-related goals.

- Learn to develop suitable policies with which to provide your board with an appropriate degree of control of the organization.

- Learn how and by what criteria to monitor and evaluate both organizational and CEO performance.

- Learn the distinctions between conventional governing boards and "workgroup" boards.

- Understand several of the basic elements essential to productive board meetings.

- Discover many of the principles of effective board organization.

- Learn why committees are important to your board and understand the relationship between committees and staff.

- Learn why a year-round leadership development effort is important to the long-term effectiveness of your board and the techniques of implementing it.

• Achieve a greater degree of satisfaction and personal growth from your experience on your board.

This book and its companion, Book II, in which I will discuss in detail the board's role in strategic planning, were designed for governing boards of directors who serve such diverse nonprofit organizations as human services agencies, cultural and arts organizations, membership organizations, environmental organizations, community development organizations, housing authorities and commissions, large organizations, small organizations, organizations with as well as without staff, and so forth. It will also help board members of such organizations as hospitals, colleges and universities, churches, and schools face the challenges involved in serving such nonprofit institutions. Much of the material will also be applicable to those who serve on service club boards, auxiliary boards, and the boards of directors of large state or national associations and, to a lesser extent, advisory boards or councils.

One word of caution: Each nonprofit organization has its own history, its own purpose and mission, its own unique culture or style, its own individual personality. Although the principles outlined herein have proven their worth in a vast spectrum of nonprofit organizations, they should never be applied rigidly or unquestioningly. Rather, you should read this book thoughtfully, with an eye toward applying its ideas and your common sense to your particular situation. In this spirit, *Building a Better Board: A Guide to Effective Leadership* should help you to improve your ability to support and guide the nonprofit organization you have so generously agreed to serve.

Titles and Terms

A few words of clarification about the titles and terms used in this volume will be appropriate. For the chief staff officer, I have chosen to use the acronym CEO (chief executive officer) rather than the more common executive director because in the majority of nonprofit organizations, the executive director is, or should be, considered the chief executive officer—*accountable to the board of directors for the performance of the whole organization.* There remains in many bylaws, however, some confusion over this point wherein the chief board officer—usually called the board president or the chairperson of the board—is designated in the bylaws as the chief executive officer. In the vast majority of nonprofit organizations, the chief board officer, by whatever title, is a volunteer, only occasionally present at the organization and hardly the person who should be charged with accountability to the board of directors for TOTAL organizational performance. Should your bylaws contain this all too common error, it should be corrected.

As to the chief board officer, this book will refer to this person as the president or board president. For our purposes this title may be considered synonymous with chairperson of the board. However, it should be noted that in many large nonprofits, the president may in fact be the full-time chief executive officer accountable to the board for organizational performance and, in this situation, the chief board officer will have the title of chairperson of the board.

The term workgroup board will be used in this book to designate a board of directors of an organization which lacks staff and where everything is done by volunteers, or an organization which has limited staff—an executive director and little else. In both cases, board members are likely to play dual roles: board member on the one hand, volunteer performing staff functions on the other. In the latter instance, this can be individual volunteering or volunteering through a committee assigned to perform functions normally performed by staff in a larger organization. Throughout this book, where appropriate, I will draw distinctions between workgroup boards and conventional governing boards which are not involved in doing staff work, as well as point out the need for precise role definitions in a workgroup board situation. For now, let me point out the necessity in a workgroup board without staff for the members of the board to distinguish when they are functioning as a board and when they are functioning as staff.

Finally, while this book uses the term board of directors, you may assume that this term is synonymous with the term board of trustees.

1 The Board and the Nonprofit Organization

Getting Started on the Right Foot

It is no accident that many of the most effective nonprofit boards provide their new board members with a variety of written materials designed to acquaint them with the goals, history, programs, staffing, financing, and so forth of the organization, and with an orientation meeting, held in advance of their first regular board meeting. If you are new to your board, I hope that you have been provided with the following:

- A copy of your organization's statement of purpose as well as its mission statement.

- Up-to-date bylaws—complete with any amendments not yet incorporated into the basic printed document.

- A written description of your organization's history and the services it provides.

- The mission-related goals for the organization, preferably set within a strategic or long-range plan.

- A copy of your board's Major Organizational Policies Manual.

- Any responsibilities of the board unique to your organization as well as a review of the fundamental responsibilities of nonprofit boards in general.

- Financial reports, e.g., budgets and actual expenditures for the most recently completed year and current year to date.

- The most recent annual report.

- Special or particularly pertinent reports and plans.

- A current organization chart showing the functions of board, staff, and volunteers.

- Minutes of board and key committees for the past six months—or more if circumstances require.

- A list of committee assignments and any other duties for all board members.

- Board member and key staff member rosters with addresses and phone numbers.

- A list of future regular board meeting dates, times, and places.

- Any appropriate publications dealing with your field of service.

Since you and your peers on the board are collectively the ultimate decision makers for the organization, it is important that you review these materials thoroughly before the new board member orientation meeting. This orientation meeting should be led by the board president with the assistance of the CEO. It should be a pleasurable event the purposes of which are to clarify the picture of the organization provided by such materials, to review issues that can best be presented orally, and to respond to whatever questions you may have.

If it is not disruptive to the organization's work, you may find it beneficial to meet some of the clients served by your organization. To facilitate your orientation, you may be asked to pair off with one of the older members of your board during your first six months. This more experienced board member would function as your mentor while you are learning your new role.

If this is your first experience as a board member and your background and experience have not yet prepared you for the role, you should not be embarrassed to ask for assistance. This book and the publications listed in the reference section are tools to help you become a more effective board member. Board development consultant/trainers provide a variety of workshops to help increase board effectiveness. Some community colleges around the country still provide board development workshops as well. Take advantage of such tools—both you and the organization you serve will be the better for it.

Getting started on the right foot will ensure that you are able to participate effectively from the beginning of your service on the board and will add to the satisfaction you should derive from this experience.

What Boards Do—Purpose and Mission

Before I can discuss the question of what boards do, two terms must be defined: purpose and mission.

These two terms are almost invariably used as synonyms. However, as was first pointed out by Cook (1987), it is useful to regard them as different yet related statements—one arising from the other. The first, the statement of purpose, should define the reasons *why* you have organized. What ultimate result is your organization expected to achieve? The focus of purpose is upon the word *why*. The mission statement, on the other hand, is concerned with *what*. What will your organization do in order to achieve this purpose? Or, to borrow from Drucker (1974), what is your business or what ought it to be? I will provide an example of each of these terms shortly.

I have often found it difficult to convince clients that making this distinction is useful—that is, until they themselves actually wrestle with these terms and develop a purpose *and* a mission for their own organizations. Suffice it to say that you may have observed or been a part of an organization which became so busy with what it was doing that it lost sight of why it was doing it—a case of the means becoming the ends! When an organization loses sight of its real reasons for existence—its *why*—it is likely to begin making decisions about what it should be doing that actually work against its ability to fulfill its primary reasons for existence. Such a situation has been the first step on the road to failure for too many nonprofit, as well as for-profit, organizations. Cook (1987) compares the purpose to a beacon that draws you, without deviation, toward your ultimate destination. An apt comparison.

Your purpose need not be unique only to your organization. It might be very large in scope—so large that no one organization could ever hope to achieve it single-handedly. For example, "to prevent deafness" is a purpose clearly beyond the ability of any single organization to accomplish. In such circumstances it will fall to your mission statement to, in effect, carve out your organization's niche within such a large purpose by detailing what you will do in the overall effort to prevent deafness. Your purpose need not be completely attainable. The purpose of preventing deafness, is, for example, most unlikely to be completely achieved in the foreseeable future, if ever.

Do not overlook the public relations value of your purpose statement, which is one of the reasons that this statement should be as succinct as possible. It should be featured on your letterhead, envelopes and all other important papers and documents. It should be on any signs and over your office door. It should appear in any location that will help tell the world who you are and why you exist as an organization.

Your board should review its purpose and its mission annually. Because of its very fundamental nature, your purpose is unlikely to change with any frequency. Yet there could come a time when a change in your organization's purpose becomes necessary. The mission, being more volatile, is more readily subject to change. Demographic, funding, cultural, political, and economic changes; new needs arising; competition and the like all can affect your mission. Thus your organization needs to review its mission annually and, once again, preferably within a strategic or long-range planning process (which will be discussed in detail in Book II).

There is a reluctance on the part of some people to become involved in change—often caused by a fear of breaking away from familiar territory, or simply not wanting to exert the necessary effort. The need for change or transition may be great, but if someone suggests that perhaps this is not quite the right time to undertake the transition, the change is put off, usually indefinitely. I would suggest to you that being involved in change or transition can add a good deal of zest to the business of being a board member and is not something to be feared. So, if your board has determined that some important change is necessary concerning your mission or its related goals, don't be afraid to undertake the change. You will do your organization a lot of good and, in the process, you will all gain a greater degree of satisfaction from your efforts. I say this to you from the experience of service on some thirty boards. My most satisfying and memorable experiences came from those in which major change or transition took place while I was a member.

Now, to answer the question of what boards do, you should know that there are three primary—we might call them bedrock—functions of a governing board of directors:

1. To establish the purpose, mission, and mission-related goals of the organization.

2. To assure that purpose, mission, and mission-related goals are achieved.

3. To think creatively—dream—about the future of the organization and to lead the organization into that better future.

It should be noted that if your board is a workgroup board it is, nonetheless, a governing board with all of the above basic governing board functions *plus* whatever staff functions it has assumed.

In the performance of these primary functions, most nonprofit governing boards of directors have eight fundamental responsibilities.

Eight Fundamental Responsibilities

Many governing boards of directors have certain responsibilities related specifically to their organization and field of service—workgroup boards in particular. If this is the case in your organization, you should know what those responsibilities are. However, with only three exceptions (which I will point out in context), all boards of directors of nonprofit organizations have eight fundamental responsibilities which you should understand clearly.

I. *Establishing and achieving the purpose and mission of the organization.*

These are a board's first and foremost responsibilities. Indeed all other responsibilities I will discuss support this first one. There is one exception to this first responsibility, however, and that is that some governing boards of directors do not *establish* the purpose and mission of their organizations. These will usually be either boards of local affiliates or chapters of national organizations, or boards of organizations whose origins lie in federal, state, or county legislation. In the former case, national headquarters will have established the purpose. In the latter case, the purpose will be mandated by the legislation which, in effect, created the organization. In both instances the individual boards can usually localize their missions somewhat, but altering the purpose is not usually within the board's power.

However, *all* governing boards must see to it that purpose and mission are achieved—and achieved at as high a level of quality as the organization's resources permit. Should those resources be insufficient, then the board, CEO, and staff must work together to find ways to develop whatever resources are needed to get the job done.

Except with a workgroup type of board (to be covered in our discussion of the sixth fundamental responsibility—appointing committees), the board itself does not do any of the actual work to achieve the purpose and mission; this is normally the responsibility of the CEO and staff. But in all cases the board has the overall responsibility to see that both the purpose and the mission are in fact achieved regardless of who does the actual work.

There is a fundamental principle of board/CEO/staff relationships that you should keep in mind: *The board is primarily responsible for determining the results that are to be achieved and the CEO and staff are responsible for developing and employing the methods necessary to achieve those results.* At the upper reaches of these two concepts—results and methods—there will be some crossover between staff and board. I will discuss this later. For now, keep this principle fixed in your mind, for it will come up many times in both this volume and in Book II.

As noted earlier, both your purpose and your mission should undergo an annual review, preferably within a strategic planning process. It is my hope in this book to persuade you that strategic planning ought to become a part of the very fabric of governance in your nonprofit organization and, in Book II, to show you how to go about it. But should your organization lack a strategic plan, this annual review of purpose and mission must be done in any event to protect your organization against the effects of whatever changes might take place in your operating environment. Remember that change does not always announce itself in obvious ways. Very often change can creep in gradually and unnoticed. Thus the need for this important annual review.

II. *Determining mission-related goals and major organizational policies.*

Once your board has determined purpose and mission, it should then break that mission down into a group of mission-related goals. Indeed, the mission statement may be made up entirely of a collection of mission-related goals. These mission-related goals become your board's results expectations for the CEO and staff. I choose to refer to them as mission-related goals rather than simply goals because there can be other goals whose orientation lies in methods. And, as we have just seen, methods are primarily the responsibility of the CEO and staff. By referring to mission-related goals we underscore the relationship of these goals to the mission and thus their development is the responsibility of your board of directors.

You should refer now to figure 1-1 where these relationships are illustrated within the concept of plan-based governance. At the top of the figure you will find the board of directors which must develop a purpose (the why of the organization), then a mission (what the organization will do), followed by a family of mission-related goals. Note the vertical dotted line connected to purpose, mission, and goals which then connects to the box below labeled CEO. This dotted line, labeled resource, reminds us that in the development of purpose, mission, and mission-related goals, the CEO and staff play an advisory role, functioning as a resource to the board and thus the CEO crosses over into the board's area of responsibility for the formulation of results which the CEO and staff will be responsible for achieving. When the CEO and staff function in this role, however, they should function *at the board's level*, concentrating upon results,

Figure 1-1. **Plan Based Governance**

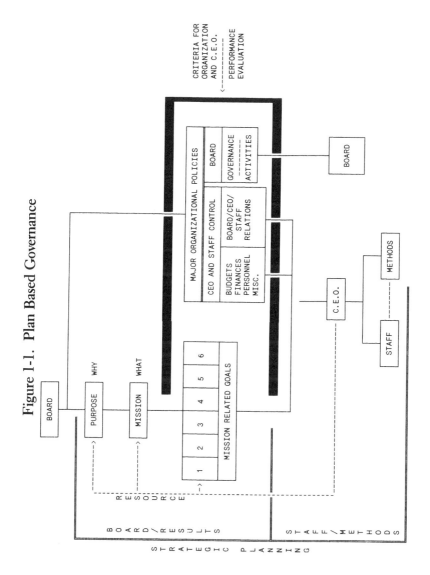

and not involve the board in staff level issues. This role is only advisory, however, for the power to make the final decisions about purpose, mission, and mission-related goals belongs only to the governing board of directors.

Note also on the outer left side of the chart a vertical double line connected to three horizontal double lines which divide the left half of the chart into upper and lower sections. Note that the outer side of this vertical line is labeled Strategic Planning. The upper section created by these double lines is labeled Board/ Results, while the lower section is labeled Staff/Methods. This is a graphic representation of a board's role in the strategic planning process. *Once your board has established the results it expects of the CEO and staff—i.e., mission-related goals—your board has completed its share of the development of the plan.* The rest of the work involved in completing the plan is all methods-oriented and is, therefore, the responsibility of your CEO and, through him or her, any other staff. A workgroup board would be an exception here since such a board will have assumed responsibility for some functions normally the responsibility of staff in a conventional governing board and will, therefore, have some responsibilities in the actual completion of the plan.

Since governing boards of directors are responsible for developing a purpose, mission, and mission-related goals for their organizations, there is no reason whatsoever why such a board of directors should not insist upon a strategic plan for its organization; the board's contribution to the plan is a byproduct of what the board must do in any event! For this reason I have chosen to call this approach to governance plan-based governance. Strategic planning ought to become a part of the very fabric of governance in your nonprofit organization.

It is often asserted that a board that doesn't plan for its future is placing that future in jeopardy. This is just as true when times are good as it is true when times are difficult. The role of the board in the strategic planning process will be discussed in considerably greater detail in Book II.

At this point some examples of purpose, mission, and mission-related goals are in order. For our examples let us assume the existence of a fictitious organization called The Literacy Program of Ghengis County. Its purpose is simple, straightforward, and leaves no doubt as to *why* the organization exists:

The purpose of The Literacy Program of Ghengis County is to eliminate illiteracy in Ghengis County.

The mission of this organization is a mission that consists of a family of mission-related goals:

In pursuit of this purpose, the mission of The Literacy Program of Ghengis County consists of the following six mission-related goals:

1. There shall be a countywide awareness of the problem of illiteracy and of the availability of help within the Program to assist individuals to learn to read.

2. Appropriate tutoring and self-help training materials shall be purchased or developed and made available for use by Program clients and tutors.

3. A cadre of *volunteer* tutors shall be recruited and trained in the techniques of teaching illiterate individuals to read.

4. The preferred ratio of tutor to student shall be *one to one*.

5. A job placement service, or guidance in seeking placements, shall be made available to graduates of the Program.

6. Fees shall be charged for tutoring services consistent with each individual's ability to pay. *No client shall be turned away due to inability to pay.*

Note that while all of these mission-related goals are stated as results to be achieved, some of them have one or both of two other characteristics: options and organizational values. Options which may be exercised by the CEO and staff appear underlined in goals 2, 4, 5, and 6. Organizational values appear *in italics* in goals 3, 4, and 6. Mission-related goals might also have other characteristics such as priorities, time lines or time frames, task assignments, and so forth depending upon the nature of the specific goal. Priorities might be expressed in numerical or chronological order of importance or as a percentage of resources to be allocated to each of several programs. When allocating percentages of resources, be sure that these percentages fall short of 100 percent to leave the CEO leeway to respond to shifting demands or conditions.

Task assignments will not normally arise at this level except with a workgroup board. In such a board, the CEO will not be held accountable for *total* organizational performance and certain functions will be carried out by board committees. A mission-related goal then might be assigned to a board committee, which is therefore accountable to the board for achieving that goal.

As with purpose and mission, your organization's mission-related goals must be subjected to an annual review as well—again, preferably, within a strategic planning process. If there is a strategic plan, you will (or should) have a formal plan book (see Book II) in which purpose, mission, and mission-related goals are kept. In the absence of a plan, the purpose, mission, and mission-related goals might be combined with the board's Major Organizational Policies Manual (discussed below).

We will now turn our attention to the board's responsibility for determining major organizational policies. Once again I have given a familiar word a prefix—major organizational policies. However, before proceeding further, a definition of the word policy is in order: *Policies are precepts or principles designed to influence and control present and future decisions, directions, and actions.*

Despite the fact that a commonly held principle in the nonprofit world is that boards make policy and the CEO and staff implement it, the lamentable fact is that few boards make any policies having to do with governance. O'Connell (1985), Houle (1989), and Carver (1990) have all taken note of the fact that few boards actually make policy, yet everyone else around them seems to! The CEO makes policies for the rest of the staff, department heads make policies for subordinates, even the janitor is likely to have policies (admittedly unwritten) as to how the floors will be swept. The only policies boards seem to commonly make are personnel policies, which, as we shall see, are better made by the CEO. By failing to make judicious use of their policy-making authority most governing boards of directors ignore what is probably their most efficacious governing tool.

I have chosen the prefix major organizational in order to distinguish the policies which governing boards ought to be making from those policies that others make. The term suggests that these are policies which one way or another tend to affect the whole organization and, as such, are the responsibility of the board. Look again at figure 1-1 and you will see another box, on the same level as mission-related goals, labeled Major Organizational Policies. You will also see that such policies are broken down into two categories: CEO & Staff Control and Board. The former are policies designed to establish certain controls upon the methods employed by the CEO and, through the CEO, the staff. The latter are policies which the board establishes for itself—for its governing activities as well as for any other activity for which the board assumes responsibility such as fund raising.

Unfortunately, many boards fail to monitor or control the activites of their CEO (they seemingly take the view that their job is simply to hire, pay, and fire!), and thus fail to live up to their fiduciary responsibilities. Such boards are open to the charge of negligence and their CEOs are consequently left in the dark as to how they stand with the board and what the board's expectations are. This is not only wrong but dangerous as well.

Other boards take their fiduciary responsibilities seriously but, unfortunately, all too frequently employ inappropriate methods in discharging these responsibilities. Such boards will be found deeply involved in budget development, financial analysis, personnel matters, and other activities which amount to micro-management of the organization—i.e., usurping the proper administrative authority of the CEO. Such activities not only frustrate the CEO but also relieve the CEO of accountability for the performance of the organization because the board has interfered in activities for which the CEO should be held accountable.

A better way is to return to what boards have always been supposed to be doing in the first place—determining policies which will help them to better govern their organizations. Your board should determine appropriate CEO and staff control policies which will provide the board with an appropriate degree of control of the organization. Carver (1990) suggests a starting point for a board in such policy making is for it to establish a sort of umbrella policy (my term) forbidding the CEO from doing anything or permitting any action that is either unethical or imprudent. If the board has said nothing else about a staff activity, that activity must at least be carried out in a prudent and ethical manner.

All well and good. A breach of ethics is not overly difficult to identify, but what about prudence—when an action that would be considered acceptable risk by one person, would seem to exceed the bounds of prudence in the view of another? Thus the board will want to establish other CEO and staff control policies in specific areas; for example:

- The CEO shall not present any budget to the board for review which fails to adequately address the purpose, mission, mission-related goals, and strategic plan of the organization.

- The CEO shall not present any budget to the board for review in which expense exceeds income.

- The CEO shall not present any budget to the board for review in which a projected deficit is eliminated by means of spending endowment principal.

- Neither the CEO nor the staff shall take any action which places the organization at financial risk.

- The CEO shall not allow the current ratio (on the balance sheet) to fall below X to Y (e.g., 2:1).

- The CEO may borrow up to $X from the special purpose fund to meet current obligations but only if the total amount borrowed will be replaced within Y days.

- The CEO shall make no single expenditure larger than X% of the operating budget without the advice and consent of the board. (This limitation ought to be set reasonably high since other CEO and staff control policies will also impinge upon spending.)

- Personnel policies established by the CEO shall be humane and equitable, shall set appropriate standards of performance for all personnel, shall be in full compliance with local, state, and federal statutes and regulations and shall be reviewed regularly by the CEO for compliance with such statutes and regulations.

- Total compensation (payroll, fringe benefits, etc.) shall not significantly exceed competitive and applicable local, regional, or national levels.

- The CEO shall immediately notify the board of any projected change or lapse of the directors and officers liability insurance.

- The CEO is accountable only to the full board of directors.

By establishing CEO and staff control policies such as these, the board can avoid becoming involved in operational details and, instead, monitor and evaluate the CEO's performance against such policies. I will discuss the monitoring role of the board later. Carver (1990) provides an extended discussion with numerous examples of these kinds of policies.

Note again figure 1-1 and the large bracket that encloses the two blocks Mission-Related Goals and Major Organizational Policies. The combination of these goals and policies establishes the criteria by which the board of directors can monitor and evaluate organizational and CEO performance. The combination of these goals and policies provides, in effect, a complete job description for the CEO: The CEO is responsible for achieving the purpose, mission, and mission-related goals established by the board of directors in a timely fashion and in so doing shall not transgress any relevant·major organizational CEO and staff control policies. Such a job description is updated automatically with every change in mission-related goals and major organizational CEO and staff control policies.

Note also that in establishing these CEO and staff control policies the board does not tell the CEO or other staff *how* to do anything. For the board to tell the CEO how to do something would be to relieve the CEO of responsibility for the outcome. For this reason, CEO and staff control policies should advise your CEO and staff of those actions which your board believes to be unacceptable.

Certain issues that are comparable or similar over which the board desires to exercise some control may arise with some frequency. Rather than have the board—in effect—continually re-approving such issues, the board should establish a policy that provides guidelines on such issues for the CEO. The board now has only to deal with the exceptions.

Your board should not overdo in this area of determining CEO and staff control policies. To overdo in this area is to return the board to micromanagement of the organization—the very problem we are attempting to eliminate through this use of policy. As in all things, use common sense in your policy making.

The second category of major organizational policies are those that are the board's own. For example:

- The board president after consultation with the CEO and with each board committee chair shall plan the agenda for each meeting of the board of directors. The board by its majority vote may alter the agenda as a first order of business at any board meeting.

- At any special meeting of the board, the board shall not act upon any issue not specified in the agenda for the special meeting provided with the notice of the special meeting, unless every member of the board is present at the time the unspecified issue is discussed and voted upon.

In Part 2, the section that deals with individual responsibilities of board members, you will note several of these individual responsibilities that could also be established as board policy for your board.

Major organizational policies established by the board of directors should not simply be included in the minutes. Policies buried in the minutes quickly become nonpolicies! There should be a Major Organizational Policies Manual containing only those major organizational policies determined by your governing board of directors. Policies and procedures set by others should not be included. And, as with purpose, mission, and mission-related goals, your board's major organizational policies should be reviewed annually. I recommend that your board assign this review of policies to the various committees that recommended them. Such a committee should conduct its review on the anniversary date of the policy or of its last review and then recommend to the board that the policy either be reaffirmed, canceled or altered in some way.

When the board adopts mission-related goals or major organizational policies three steps are involved:

1. *Formulation:* This activity begins with the initial suggestion; continues to include whatever study, review, and
   deliberation the suggestion is subjected to—probably in a
   committee; and concludes with, preferably, optional recommendations. Anyone who is appropriately involved
   with the goal or policy under discussion ought to be able
   to play an appropriate role in formulating the recommendations: board members, the CEO, other staff members,
   clients, client representatives, community representatives,
   consultants, and so forth. You should never cut yourself off
   from any resource that can be useful to your board's
   decision making.

2. *Determination:* This is the point of decision and with
   mission-related goals and major organizational policies,
   only the board of directors has the authority to make the
   final decision.

3. *Implementation:* In most cases implementation is the responsibility of staff, unless the board says it is not. In the
   latter case usually the workgroup style of board would have
   others besides staff carrying out board decisions. (Workgroup boards will be discussed further under "Appointing
   committees.")

When writing goals or policies, be brief. Goals and policies
should be stated clearly and succinctly, uncluttered with procedures, and always put in writing. The board should agree at the
time of determining a goal or policy upon the precise language
to be used and then verify that the secretary has recorded the
policy or goal in the *exact* words specified by the board. Never
leave the final wording of such important board pronouncements
up to the secretary's memory. The risk of words that might alter
the board's intent slipping into a policy or goal statement is too
great.

In summary these first two fundamental responsibilities are
primary. By establishing the purpose, mission, and mission-

related goals, the board thereby clarifies for the CEO and staff the board's results expectations. These goals, together with the major organizational CEO and staff control policies, collectively become the criteria by which the board will monitor and evaluate organizational as well as CEO performance. Because this approach to governance will eliminate the seeming necessity for your board to become involved in details that should really be the responsibility of your CEO, your board will be better able to devote its energies to those other things boards are supposed to be doing: in particular, thinking creatively—dreaming—about your organization's future and leading it into that better future.

III. *Raising and managing the organization's funds.*

I am frequently disappointed to hear board members assert that fund raising is really the job of the CEO. If by fund raising we mean such things as obtaining allocations from United Way, federal or state subsidies or reimbursements, fees for services, program-related foundation grants, then, yes, fund raising from such sources is best left to the CEO and/or a designated subordinate, with board support when needed. But if your organization is going to raise money from the community in annual giving programs or capital campaigns, then fund raising usually becomes the responsibility of the board. Successful fund raising from the community is usually best done by peers in the community with CEO and staff support. Even in large organizations with a development office and staff, the board should play a major role in making contacts and opening doors as well as major solicitations. In smaller organizations lacking development staff, the burden of fund raising from the community falls entirely to the board for, in most cases, the CEO lacks the time, contacts, and temperament to do a proper job of raising substantial funds from the community.

It should be noted that fund *raising* as such is not governance. It is an activity for which a board assumes responsibility. However, your board's relationship to funds becomes governance

1) because the board is responsible for seeing that sufficient funds—regardless of the source—are raised to carry out the organization's purpose, and 2) when the board assumes its fiduciary responsibility of assuring that all organizational funds are properly and prudently managed. As has already been noted, this fiduciary responsibility will be best discharged by setting appropriate CEO and staff control policies in the financial area and then monitoring CEO performance against those policies. We will discuss the board's monitoring function shortly.

IV. *Employing the staff.*

A governing board of directors is responsible for hiring, monitoring, evaluating, compensating, and, if necessary, terminating only one employee in the organization:—the CEO. Indeed, to have the board involved in any of these activities with staff below the level of CEO is to relieve the CEO of accountability for the quality of the staff and organizational performance in general. However, your board does function as the ultimate employer of all staff by:

- Assuring that personnel policies established by the CEO are humane, equitable, legal, and in accordance with your board's CEO and staff control policies concerning personnel policies.

- Assuring that compensation paid to employees complies with whatever policies your board has established with respect to compensation.

- Approving major fringe benefit programs such as health care and retirement plans since the providers of such plans will usually require a board resolution approving the plan.

- Functioning, through an ad hoc committee set up for the purpose, as a grievance committee in what should normally be the rare event of an employee grievance which cannot be resolved at a lower level in the organization.

It goes without saying that if your organization has no staff and all the work is done by volunteers, this fundamental board responsibility will not apply to your organization. However, should you grow and eventually hire your first CEO and, perhaps, other staff, do not forget to add this responsibility to the others you already have.

V. *Monitoring and evaluating the performance of the CEO.*

With the establishment of mission-related goals and the determination of CEO and staff control policies, the board has, in effect, written the job description for the CEO and established those criteria by which the CEO's performance will be monitored and evaluated. Should your board be a workgroup board it should monitor and evaluate the performance of the volunteers who function individually or in committees in lieu of staff. This monitoring and evaluation is, for the most part, an ongoing process consisting of five activities:

1. Paying close attention to the CEO's regular reports to the board, both written and oral.*

2. Review of the CEO's proposed budget and subsequent comparison of regular financial reports against that budget.*

3. Periodic review of CEO and staff compliance with established CEO and staff control policies by ad hoc board committees or by outside expertise, paid or volunteer, brought in for the purpose.

4. By keeping your eyes and ears open and being aware of what is taking place within the organization.

5. The annual evaluation of CEO performance.

---

*In organizations lacking staff, these would be committee reports.

Few boards can get the job done by meeting less than monthly so your CEO will likely be called upon to report monthly to your board of directors. There ought to be both a written as well as an oral report at the meeting itself.

The written report should present whatever facts and statistics are routinely reported to your board each month as a sort of index of activity. For example: so many admissions, so many discharges, so many season tickets sold, so many in attendance at the last concert, so many meals served, and so forth. Most such reports are better read than heard so this report should be mailed to board members together with the other materials that should be mailed to them in advance of the board meeting such as the next meeting's agenda, minutes, financial report and so forth.

The formal report of the CEO to your board should be oral and its principal features should be recorded in the minutes. By making it an oral report, it can be as current as the last minute before the board meeting. This report should focus upon:

- Progress, or its lack, toward achieving mission-related goals.

- With a strategic plan in place, the report should reference key steps within the plan.

- Successes the organization has enjoyed over the reporting period.

- Potential problems which will eventually come to the board's attention. Since few boards welcome unpleasant surprises, the sooner potential problems are made known, the better.

- Education of the board with respect to the field of service. This could come in written form as well.

- Miscellaneous items such as trends developing, new needs arising, sharing information sent from a national association, and so forth.

When planning the agenda, allow a reasonable amount of time for this important report. In the event that anything in this report will affect another item on the board's agenda, the report should be placed in an appropriate position on the agenda. In no event should this important report be scheduled as the last item on the agenda.

It can also be beneficial for your board to hear occasional reports from other staff members about their particular areas of responsibility. Not only will this help your board better understand what is happening, it is also a good educational experience for subordinate staff members to be exposed to a board of directors.

In the area of budgets and finances, I have previously suggested several possible CEO and staff control policies that a board might establish. Your CEO is responsible for developing a proposed budget for the organization's coming year. This budget should be reviewed by the board; however, board members should keep their collective eyes on the big picture and not attempt to descend into minutiae. The budget should be examined in terms of the policies the board may have set relative to the budget. For example: Does the budget appear to adequately address purpose, mission, mission-related goals, and strategic plan? Are income projections conservative? Is the budget balanced? Is the board's projected contribution to income from its fund raising on target?

Well-established custom notwithstanding, a board should refrain from *approving* the budget for the simple reason that its members are not sufficiently knowledgeable about operations to do so—and have no way of acquiring such detailed knowledge without considerable disruption to the organization. To approve the budget is to accept at least some responsibility for its adequacy and, if a board wishes to hold its CEO responsible for all of the details involved in total organizational performance, it should not approve the budget. If a budget meets the tests of your board's budget-related CEO and staff control policies, then the board should simply accept it and return it to the CEO with the understanding that it is the CEO's responsibility to make it work. Should your board find the budget unacceptable in one or more ways, it should exercise its veto power and return the proposed budget to the CEO to be reworked. Exceptions to this would be agencies controlled by county or state government where the board is required to approve the agency's operating budget.

A similar approach, based upon appropriate CEO and staff control policies, should be taken to the review of financial reports. Questions such as "Why were office supply expenses so high last month?" are really not a concern of the board unless there has been a history of excess in this account over a longer period. Similarly, board approval of bills to be paid is an archaic practice and a waste of a board's time. (However, once again, such a practice may be required of some agencies by state or county government.)

In reviewing financial reports, your board's eyes should be on the larger picture. For example: does the report track the budget reasonably well overall? Is income coming in as predicted? Is the current ratio at or above the required minimum level? Has the loan from the special purpose fund taken out two months ago because of a momentary cash flow problem been repaid on time? Are your accounts payable current? Are your IRS withholding payments current? And, of course, there should be an annual audit of the books done by an outside accounting firm. Such an audit not only ensures good accounting practices, but should also verify compliance with your board's CEO and staff control policies in the financial area.

Many if not most boards of directors use a finance committee to review financial reports in advance of their submission to the full board. With a small board whose members are reasonably comfortable reviewing financial reports, this committee is probably a redundancy. However, if many board members are inexperienced in reviewing such reports, a finance committee may be desirable to assist the board in financial reviews as well as to recommend CEO and staff control policies in the financial area.

It is important to bear in mind, however, that the finance committee should review financial reports against the board's CEO and staff control policies and not become engrossed in minute detail or usurp the CEO's financial responsibilities. The existence of an endowment might also justify a finance committee to oversee the work of the bank or asset management company that has been engaged to manage that endowment. It would be unwise for a finance committee to actually attempt to manage an endowment portfolio as committees cannot act as speedily as professional management in a volatile market.

If you are inexperienced in reviewing financial reports, do not be embarrassed to ask for help. If you do not understand the report, it is likely that others are in the same boat. Your failure to understand the financial report will not relieve you of your share of responsibility with all of the other board members for the financial integrity of your organization. It is, therefore, imperative that you understand this important report.

From time to time compliance with other CEO and staff control policies established by your board should be monitored. This can be done either by small ad hoc committees of the board or by outside expertise (paid or pro bono) such as is done with the annual audit of the books. For example, compliance of the organization's personnel policies and practices with the board's CEO and staff control policies on personnel policies can be monitored in this way. Similarly your organization's compensation plans can be reviewed for compliance with the board's CEO and staff control policies on compensation.

The findings of such committees or outside experts as to CEO compliance with board policies should be reported directly to the board of directors. Such committees or outside experts should not dictate to the CEO, however; only the board of directors may give direction to the CEO.

In a similar vein:

Occasionally a CEO will encounter a problem which he or she will need to talk out with someone. Board members,

those with knowledge and skills in the problem area in
particular, should be ready and willing to listen, discuss and
offer counsel. But in offering counsel, board members—
including the president—must not expect that their advice
must be taken, because the final decision must lie with the
CEO. If it is otherwise, the board cannot then hold its CEO
accountable for the result. [Swanson, 1990, D-64.]

Keeping one's eyes and ears open while at or in touch with the
organization is another source of information available to board
members. However, this is not an invitation to meddle! Indeed,
to have board members discussing CEO performance with any
subordinate staff is entirely out of order and can be seriously
disruptive to an organization. In the same vein if you are
approached by a friend on the staff who has a complaint and
seeks your assistance, you must politely but firmly refer this
person to the CEO or, if that is not acceptable, to the grievance
process in the personnel policies. But do keep your eyes and ears
open and notice such things as how the phone is being answered,
whether employee turnover is normal or abnormally high, the
apparent state of employee morale, and so forth. If subordinate
staff are assigned as committee support, what caliber of support
is being provided? Such observations may lead to questions that
should be raised during the annual performance evaluation.
The fifth monitoring tool available to your board is the annual
performance evaluation of the CEO. Some argue that if mission-
related goals are in place, if major organizational control policies
exist, and if the board is monitoring performance in an ongoing
fashion as discussed above, then the annual performance evaluation is really redundant. I disagree with this position for several
reasons. It is all too easy for board members to monitor and yet
fail to communicate to the CEO, and for the record, their
summary estimate of the quality of the CEO's performance. Any
CEO has an absolute right to know how he or she stands with
the board of directors. To stop once a year and formally review

performance against established criteria ensures that a *formal record* of the board's view of the CEO's performance is being maintained. This formal record is necessary to protect both sides. It protects the CEO from an impulsive board which might suddenly decide to terminate the CEO's employment without the prior warning a series of marginal or poor evaluations would have provided. It protects the board should it decide to terminate the CEO because it has developed a documented history of successive evaluations leading to and supportive of its decision to terminate the CEO's employment.

The annual evaluation should not attempt to evaluate any activity for which criteria have not existed over the period being evaluated. I have detailed a process for the annual CEO performance evaluation based upon mission-related goals and major organizational CEO and staff control policies (Swanson, 1992). Please refer to the reference section for further information.

Unfortunately few boards conduct a useful annual performance evaluation of their CEOs. Many believe the process to be inherently negative—which it should not be—because the word evaluation implies criticism. Performance evaluation should imply constructive criticism as well as constructive praise. Another obstacle to good performance evaluations is the general lack of useful information about how to go about the process. Too many recommended evaluation processes are unnecessarily complex and time-consuming. A third obstacle, of course, is the failure of many boards to establish the necessary criteria: purpose, mission, mission-related goals, and major organizational CEO and staff control policies. Nevertheless, the CEO has a right to know where he or she stands with respect to the board and the board needs to be able to base its opinion of its CEO on solid, demonstrated, and documented fact. The annual, formal performance evaluation is, therefore, an important responsibility for most governing boards of directors.

When discussing the board's responsibility to monitor and evaluate the CEO's performance, some words should also be said about the board's responsibility to support its CEO. Until such time as a board determines it must replace its CEO, the board should always entirely support its CEO publicly. Any criticism of the CEO should be kept within the family and not put on public view. To do otherwise is to present an unattractive view of the organization to the public and potential donors and, in certain fields, such activity can have a devastating effect upon clients dependent in one way or another upon the organization.

VI. *Appointing committees.*

Contrary to the many cynical jokes about the usefulness of committees, it is a rare board that can function without the help of appropriate committees. The primary function of board committees is to reduce the workload of the board. Should your full board attempt to deal with all of the detail surrounding every decision it must make, its members would soon be bogged down in that detail.

Board committees study, review, deliberate, and then recommend options to the board for final decision. While optional recommendations are not always possible or sensible, your board should not have to consider just a single recommendation from a committee. In most instances, committees have no power to make final decisions unless the board grants that power in a particular situation. In some states, however, nonprofit law does give certain committees the power to act for the board. With the exception of the executive committee's power to act for the board in a bona fide emergency as discussed in part 5, this is a provision I heartily disapprove of. You should review your state's nonprofit laws on this point.

The term subcommittee is often used when committee is the correct word. A subcommittee is a committee that reports to another committee. The usual rationale for a subcommittee is to reduce the number of committees that report directly to the board. This situation would normally only be found with a workgroup type of board. For example, a program committee might have a subcommittee under it to take charge of running a specific event.

It is the board president's responsibility to make the committee chair appointments as well as committee member appointments. The president's choices—at least for the committee chair appointments—should receive the approval of the full board. In making his or her recommendation, the president must evaluate the needs of each committee and evaluate the competencies of the available people. Then the president must make sure that each committee gets its fair and appropriate share of the available talent from among the board and, where permissible, from among nonboard people.

Board committees are an ideal training ground for future board members. In part 4 I will detail a system of identifying potential board members. If you can make use of such people on one or more of your board committees, they will learn a good bit about your organization thus giving them a head start should you eventually invite them to join the board. The reverse is also true. Your board can observe how well these nonboard committee members perform in their committee assignments and, if they fail to measure up, then the board is warned that such persons would probably not be good board members. As a board member you should try to get a variety of committee assignments during your tenure. This will make your experience as a board member more interesting and such variety in your committee experience is excellent preparation for higher office.

Four common *board* committees, all concerned with governance, are executive, nominating, finance, and strategic planning. The first three are discussed elsewhere in this book and the strategic planning committee or, as it is sometimes called, the planning team is discussed in Book II. A fifth board committee, fund raising, is not concerned with governance as noted on p. 27. These committees should be specified in the bylaws with a brief charge detailing their responsibilities and composition. Other committees which your board might need only occasionally should be considered ad hoc committees—i.e., temporary committees that exist only until their charge has been completed. Membership on the executive and nominating committees should be restricted to board members, but all other committees ought to be open to nonboard members whenever appropriate. Remember that using some nonboard people on board committees can enable an organization to reduce the size of its board.

Some committees are not concerned with governance; rather they are involved in activities normally reserved for staff in larger organizations. This is the distinguishing characteristic of what has been previously defined as a workgroup board. Such committees may include both board and nonboard members. Committees such as program, activities, newsletter, buildings and grounds, and ticket sales are examples of those committees which do work typically assigned to staff in larger organizations, or those which assist staff in staff activities.

In organizations having at least a CEO the workgroup style of board can become problematical. The difficulty lies in who is to be accountable and for what. Should your board assume full responsibility for an activity normally performed by paid staff, then the committee should look to the board for direction and the CEO should be relieved of accountability for whatever this committee does. This committee is, therefore, a committee of a workgroup board. It is essential that if your board is a workgroup type of board, responsibilities and accountability must be clearly worked out, assigned, and scrupulously observed. A lack of clarity in definition of responsibilities and accountability can be the source of serious difficulties between the board and the CEO.

On the other hand, if the board wishes to hold the CEO accountable for total organizational performance, then the committee or group of volunteers doing work which would normally be done by paid staff, and for which the CEO is therefore responsible, must act under the supervision and control of the CEO. If you as a board member serve on such a committee or as a volunteer, your board member status is temporarily suspended because in this setting you are simply a volunteer. This will not, therefore, be a workgroup board and such a committee would not be a committee of the board. The choice of volunteers to serve on such committees is up to the CEO or the CEO's designated subordinate. However, the board could assist in identifying possible volunteers or members for such committees.

VII. *Holding property.*
Your organization's property may include real estate, tools, rolling stock, equipment, endowment, and so forth. This responsibility also extends to such things as the protection against loss of important data—mail lists, donor lists, financial records. Regardless of who actually does the work of maintaining and caring for the organization's property, your board of directors is ultimately responsible for whatever your organization owns, leases, or has free use of and must, therefore, periodically assure itself that such maintenance, care, and protection is being provided.

VIII. *Leadership development.*
The quality of your board of directors will ultimately determine the quality of the services or products your organization provides. Therefore, the board must have a year-round leadership development program to guarantee that your organization will not come up short when your board needs new members. In part 4 I will discuss a system for identifying, recruiting, nominating, electing, and developing new board members.

2 You and Your Board

Individual Board Member Responsibilities

All of the responsibilities we have just discussed apply to your board *functioning as a whole*. But you, as an individual, have certain important responsibilities as well. You must be willing to attend and participate in most, if not all, of your board's meetings, as well as those of the committee(s) to which you have been assigned. You should be willing to serve actively on at least one active committee. You must be willing to do the homework involved. For board and committee meetings to be well run and efficient, participants must study the materials sent out in advance, especially those concerning issues that will require action at the meeting. Finally, as a member of the board you have the obligation to support your organization financially when it goes fund raising—*within your means*. It is expected that board members will place the organization on whose board they sit at, or very near, the top of their personal philanthropic priorities.

These individual responsibilities constitute the minimum commitment individual board members must bring to their offices. The effectiveness of your board depends heavily upon all of its members being willing to make at least this level of commitment. There are some other important individual responsibilities as well.

Action by Individual Members

To begin with, the board acts only as a whole and individual board members lack the authority to act unilaterally. This is true of every aspect of board membership. No individual board member, including the board president, may take any kind of action that can be construed as an act of the full board without the expressed sanction of the full board of directors. This means, among other things, that individual board members do not speak for the board unless authorized to do so. This caveat is especially important when the media are involved. Typically, the board president and the CEO will be the only persons authorized to speak for the organization and its board publicly. (An exception might be when a board member who is experienced in dealing with the media is delegated to act as the media spokesperson.) If you are ever in doubt about whether your public statements will be taken solely as your own and not interpreted as the word of the board, the best advice I can offer is *don't!*

At times your board may make a decision with which you disagree and may even have voted against. Should you be in this position, you must remember that, publicly, you must support this decision or at the least remain silent. As a board member you are a member of a team and when the team makes its decision, it has a right to expect *all* of its members to support that decision. Of course, within the board you are free to continue to fight for your position. Indeed, if you feel strongly enough about the issue, as a conscientious board member you have an obligation to do just that. But your disagreement must be kept within the board. However, should the decision be one that you cannot in good conscience support, and you feel you must speak out publicly against it, then you must first resign from your board and work for change from the outside.

Your board must always give the outside world the impression of unity. A publicly divided board looks bad to the clients your organization serves, and a publicly divided board is a poor candidate for philanthropy. Also, a divided board—whose members lack the personal discipline to abide by majority vote and subordinate personal differences for the good of the organization—is bound to be an *ineffective* board in the long run.

Board Members as Volunteers

Earlier we discussed the workgroup style of board where certain committees do work that would normally be assigned to staff in a larger organization. I want to bring this down to an individual level and discuss *you* in a possibly dual role—board member as well as hands-on volunteer. This has been called the two-hat syndrome and it has special potential pitfalls. For example, suppose that you are a board member of a neighborhood center and are also a ceramics teacher. As such, you occasionally volunteer to teach ceramics to center clients. In this situation, while you are teaching in the activities room, you have removed your board member "hat." You are now wearing a "volunteer" hat and you serve under the direct supervision of the activities director who reports to the very CEO who in turn is accountable to you and your peers on the board for total organizational performance—including the activities room.

This is an important distinction for you to remember for if, as a volunteer in the activities room, you attempted to throw your weight around as a board member, you would create much havoc and resentment in the organization. First, you would have given the activities director a second boss—an intolerable situation for any employee. Second, your CEO's accountability to the board of directors for performance in this area would have been compromised because you interfered.

In another case, something might occur in the activities room, with the apparent approval of the activities director, with which you, as a conscientious board member, disagree. But you have no authority to give orders or direction to the activities director. In such cases three legitimate courses of action are open to you— if you sincerely believe that something must be done.

1. You can report the incident to the CEO, *as information only*, being careful to avoid any suggestion that you are giving direction to the CEO (something that, as a single board member, you are not empowered to do). The CEO may then take whatever action seems appropriate, including doing nothing. The activities director's action may have been entirely correct, but, as a nonprofessional, this was not apparent to you.

2. You can report the incident to your board president who can (a) bring it to the attention of the CEO (also as information only), or (b) should the board president agree with you that the action was improper and the CEO has done nothing about it, bring it up at the next board meeting.

3. You can bring the matter up personally at the next board meeting.

Once the issue has reached the full board, its members have the authority to take whatever action it deems appropriate. However, before the full board acts in such a situation, it should carefully consider how deeply it wants to get its hands *into* the organization, rather than keeping its hands *on* the organization, where its hands belong. A board made up of nonprofessionals which takes issue with the professional judgment of its CEO might be making a serious mistake.

To sum up then, no board member—including the board president—or committee has the authority to unilaterally direct the activity of any staff member—including the CEO. Only the full board, acting as a whole, has the power to give direction to the CEO who, in turn, will give direction to any subordinate staff.

The President's Role

One day you may occupy the office of board president. Even if you do not, you will need to work with this important officer. Therefore, you should understand the role of the board president and the several activities for which the president is responsible.

The board of directors should be regarded as a leadership team and the president as its captain. If you are the president, you stir the pot and stimulate activity. As president, you preside at meetings of the board, the corporation, or the members. You evaluate all of the board members and other available volunteers and, with the board's approval, give them appropriate committee assignments. As president, it is your task to lead the board through the organizational year.

Be careful of the word leadership, however. A president's primary role is to get the very best out of the leadership *team* by making the best possible committee assignments, obtaining full board participation in discussions that precede decisions, and so forth. The old image of the stalwart, square-jawed "leader" who calls all the shots is, fortunately, dead. Today's organizations look for full group participation in the board's decision-making process. One of the president's most important tasks is to make this happen. Of course, there may be occasions when the board president must take a strong position on an issue, but this should be the exception, not the rule.

Now let's take a look at some of your presidential activities.

- You take the lead in orientation of new board members.

- You evaluate all of the players and, with the board's approval, make suitable committee assignments accordingly.

- You delegate what can properly be delegated in order to spread the workload and provide leadership experience for others.

- You plan ahead and know well in advance what must be done—and when—for the full year ahead.

- You make contact at least monthly, usually well before board meetings, with all of the committee chairs to ensure that their assignments are being carried out and to determine their needs at the upcoming board meeting.

- You meet with the CEO and plan the agenda for the next board meeting.

- You preside at meetings of the board and of the corporation.

- You constantly stimulate the board's leadership development efforts.

- You continue to evaluate all of the players in order to know who is performing well and who poorly, thereby predicting the future needs of the board.

- You play a leading role, possibly *the* leading role, in fund-raising efforts.

- You represent the voluntary leadership of the organization to groups within the community as well as to the community at large.

Nason (1982) puts it very well when he says,

> . . . the chairman must moderate as well as lead—a healer of breaches, harmoniser of divisiveness, sometimes cajoler

and, when necessary, a disciplinarian. To the public the chairman is the symbol of the board and very often its spokesman. Within the board the chairman sets the example for the other trustees by his or her personal performance.

And it is this last point, that of setting the example, that in the end is probably the most important.

Legal and Moral Implications

As a member of a governing board of directors, you should be aware that the responsibilities we have discussed in this book are not only moral, but many of them can be regarded as legal. Board members are not free of personal liability, although exposure to liability varies greatly from one field of service to another. Where such exposure is greater, many organizations carry directors and officers liability insurance to protect their board members in the event of legal action. Nonprofit board members have been held personally liable in legal actions against nonprofit organizations. To ascertain your own degree of exposure, you should consult your organization's legal counsel.

It should be noted that a number of states have passed legislation limiting liability of nonprofit board members and volunteers. While such legislation is commendable, it would probably be unwise to rely solely upon its existence and drop your directors and officers liability coverage. Until such legislation has stood the test of several court challenges, its protection may not be reliable. Once again, you must consult your legal counsel for advice in this important area.

As a board member, you must also be aware of any potential for conflict of interest and should guard against any situation that could involve you in such a conflict. Your bylaws very likely contain language forbidding conflicts of interest on the part of your board members. Conflict of interest can come in a variety of ways: obtaining business from the organization without com-petitive bids; as the parent of a child receiving services from the organization, attempting to obtain more favorable treatment for your child than is given other clients; as a representative on your board of an agency that receives services from your organization, trying to obtain more than what would be that agency's fair share of total services provided; and so forth. Not only would a conflict of interest be unethical, it might very well be illegal.

Board members of nonprofit organizations usually serve with-out monetary compensation. As a board member, you may receive reimbursement for extraordinary expenses. You (or a close friend or relative) may *not* receive favored treatment when there is business to be done. Should you be in the position of doing business with the organization you serve as a board member, all dealings must be open and aboveboard and should also be on a competitive bid basis. You should abstain from any involvement in the discussion about or vote on any decision from which you might benefit financially or in any other way. (Indeed, it is best if you are not present.) Once again, the best advice here is when in doubt—don't!

3 A Meeting Checklist

The greater part of your time as a member of the board of directors will be spent in meetings of the board or of the committee(s) on which you serve. It is in meetings of *committees* that issues are wrestled with and recommendations are formulated; it is in meetings of the *full board* where things all come together and decisions are made. Thus, you should know the various elements that lead to productive meetings and your role in those elements from three perspectives—as board and/or committee member, as committee chair, and as board president.

Good Meetings Begin at Home

As noted earlier, one of your personal responsibilities as a member of the board or of a committee is to do your homework. A prerequisite to any productive meeting is that all of the participants are preeducated, well in advance of the meeting, about the issues they will be dealing with at that meeting. You have an obligation to review all of the materials sent to you in advance. Waiting until the meeting itself to read these materials is not fair to the other members, or yourself.

Among the materials that should usually be sent to board members in advance of *committee* meetings are minutes of the previous meeting, the upcoming meeting's agenda, reports or studies made by staff or others which will bear upon the committee's deliberations, proposals from outside sources, and so forth.

In advance of a *full board* meeting you should receive minutes of the last meeting (these mailed within ten days of the meeting they record), the agenda for the upcoming meeting, the current financial report, the previously mentioned CEO's written (statistical index of activity) report, minutes of committee meetings held since the last board meeting packet was mailed, committee recommendations for board action accompanied by adequate (but not overdone) backup material summarizing the positive and negative aspects of the recommendations, and so forth.

If you chair one of your board's committees or serve as president of your board, you will be responsible for making sure that committee or board members receive whatever materials will help prepare them for the meeting. In the interests of making meetings more productive—as well as shorter—you should periodically exhort your committee or board members to do their homework.

About the Minutes

If possible, the minutes of the last board meeting should be mailed within ten days of that meeting so that the participants will receive them while the meeting is still reasonably fresh in their minds. The minutes ought not to be held for mailing with the notice of the next board meeting.

The minutes ought to be as brief as good communications will allow. Begin with a list of those present at the meeting and follow with a second paragraph listing those who were absent. (One of my clients has an absentee board member's name marked with a yellow highlighter on that absentee member's copy of the min-

utes just to underscore the fact that his/her absence was noticed.)
Use plain language and break the information into new paragraphs frequently. It can facilitate the board's follow-up process
if all decisions reached, including any task assignments and time
frames, are summarized at the beginning or at the end of the
minutes. Items on this follow-up list should be carried forward
in subsequent sets of minutes until the board no longer needs
the follow-up reminder. Only the full board should make the
decision to drop any item from this follow-up list.

As to the content of the minutes, the test is that they should
provide an absentee board member with a reasonable sense of
what took place and, in particular, the rationale(s) underlying
each decision that was made. The names of those who made and
seconded motions should be noted. If there was a split vote, the
number of yeas, nays, and any abstentions should be noted. If
any members ask to be recorded as to their vote or abstention,
the secretary must honor such a request.

It is desirable to have a staff person other than the CEO
actually take the minutes at the meeting thus relieving the
secretary and the CEO to participate more actively. The secretary
should check the minutes for accuracy, however. Be certain that
any decision made by the board be recorded in the exact language
used by the board at the meeting. Finally master copies of all
minutes should be maintained in a minute book which is *never*
allowed to leave the organization's office.

Planning the Agenda

Agenda planning is crucial to productive meetings, not only to
accomplish all of the necessary work, but also to develop a group
that works well together. If you chair a committee, your agenda
planning is not complicated. Typically, you will talk with any
committee member who has an assignment that must be completed in advance of the next committee meeting as well as touch

base with the committee staff support person to learn of any developments that may have taken place since the last meeting. You will then plan the actual agenda, which staff will send to committee members with the notice of the meeting. If the agenda is varied or contains controversial elements, then you, as the committee chair, should note the comments below concerning agenda dynamics for meetings of the full board.

A major responsibility of the board president is planning the agenda for the board meeting with the CEO. Between board meetings the president should be in contact with any committee chairs whose committees are active. Committee meetings should be scheduled sufficiently in advance of the full board meeting so that their minutes can be prepared and sent to all board members with the notice of the board meeting. When committees have only progress to report, doing so through their minutes will save time at the board meeting itself. However, committees that have recommendations to be acted upon by the full board or that need the board to help them in their deliberations will have to educate the board about the issues involved beforehand. The president should help each committee chair determine whether or not the committee's minutes are adequate to this task or whether additional materials—such as an explanatory memorandum from the committee chair—should be sent out to the full board.

The president of the board should meet in person (preferably) or by phone with the CEO to plan the actual agenda. The CEO will have issues to raise at the board meeting; there may be unfinished business to complete or to follow up on; there may be new business to consider; there may be groups or delegations that could not be dealt with by a committee and that must meet with the full board. All of these agenda items must be sorted out and placed in logical order for board consideration.

Whether they originate with a committee or with staff, a list of any *decisions* that will be required of the board should be printed on the agenda in appropriate order.

If you are organizing an agenda, you should pay attention to some basic group dynamics. For example, never begin a meeting with a controversial issue; to do so might set an acrimonious tone for the rest of the meeting. Similarly, ending with a controversial issue risks having participants leave the board meeting with bad feelings that can follow heavy, possibly heated, discussion. Whenever possible, a board meeting should end with discussion of an upbeat issue on which all participants can agree—preferably with some pleasure and pride. Let them leave feeling good about the organization.

If your agenda contains one or more weighty or controversial issues, place them in the middle of the agenda, not only for the reasons above, but also because you will have the maximum number of people present at this time—latecomers having arrived and early departees still present. With more than one controversial issue, separate them on the agenda by dealing with one or more issues of lesser import.

In organizing the agenda, you should pay attention to logical grouping of the components of your board meeting. For example, if your CEO's oral report will shed light on an issue to be taken up by the board, place the CEO's report first.

Once the president and the CEO have completed the agenda, it is ready to be sent out with the other materials going out to each board member along with the notice of the meeting. This packet should be mailed approximately seven to ten days in advance of the meeting, if the meeting is a regularly scheduled one (e.g., always the third Wednesday of every month at 7:00 P.M.). If the meeting is not regularly scheduled, as is often the case with committees, then ten days to two weeks is more appropriate.

General Robert and His Rules

If you are chairing a meeting of a committee or your board, you should remember that *Robert's Rules of Order* were developed initially for large parliamentary bodies, and their rigid application may inhibit the kind of give-and-take which should characterize your board and committee meetings. A board that enthusiastically applies *Robert's Rules*—that crosses every parliamentary "t" and dots every parliamentary "i"—is often a group of people who are not working well together and require a very formal structure to facilitate their deliberations. Varying degrees of formality will be required in your board and committee meetings; therefore, you should use common sense in your application of *Robert's Rules*. Of course, at meetings of members, large associations, conventions, open meetings, and the like, *Robert's Rules* must be followed with greater diligence.

At the Meeting

Individual participants in a meeting all have some responsibilities to the group as a whole which, if met, will help in making the meeting productive. You should consider the following simple checklist of such responsibilities.

- Do your homework.

- Be sensitive to any cultural differences that may exist among the participants and refrain from judging people of other cultures by the standards of your own.

- Show respect for the others—even when you disagree.

- *Listen* to what the others have to say.

- Do not reject ideas out of hand. Even the wildest idea might stimulate a train of thought that goes somewhere.

- Do not dominate—rather, participate to a reasonable degree.

• And men should remember that they have no corner on knowledge, wisdom, and experience!

In the Chair

If you find yourself chairing a meeting of a committee or a full board of directors, you should be sure to *start on time*. If there is a quorum present at the appointed hour, bring the meeting to order and get under way. Catering to those who seem incapable of being on time for any event is a tacit invitation to everyone to be late. Generally, when a pattern of beginning on time has been established, most of the group will make the effort to be on time. Note: meetings generally need to start on time to end on time.

The degree of leadership which you must exercise over the proceedings again will vary with the type of meeting and the work to be accomplished. If you chair a brainstorming session of the strategic planning committee, your job will be simply to guide the discussion loosely, see that everyone participates, that no one dominates, and that no ideas are criticized. If you chair a formal meeting of the board of directors and a number of important decisions need to be made, your leadership will follow more formal lines. One thing, however, is common to all meetings you will chair—your job is to get the best that you can from everyone in the group.

As chair you should see that everyone participates and that a few do not dominate. Most boards or committees have unassertive members, some of whom may well be capable of providing the idea that saves the day—if you can get them involved in the discussion. One way to involve such people is to "go-round-the-table." Start with the person on your left, giving each person, say, fifteen seconds to state where he or she stands on the issue under discussion. Along the way you will pick up the opinions of your least assertive members who might be reluctant to speak if you chose to single them out instead.

This technique can also solve the problem of a committee or board member who remains silent at the meeting, but has much to say after the meeting has adjourned—most of it critical. "Going-round-the-table" forces such a person to speak for the record or remain silent, either of which will tend to minimize the impact of that person's "coatroom" criticism.

People who talk too much can also be a problem for you as the chair, and impatience is rarely the answer. An approach that will work often enough to justify the effort is to try to become more closely acquainted with such persons and to build a bridge of confidence with them. By doing so you can sometimes learn how to signal them that their point has been made and that it will receive fair treatment in your hands.

People who criticize or put down others are another problem. If one of your board or committee members is put down by another, you, as chair, must come to the rescue. As soon as possible, draw this person back into the discussion with reassurances that his or her point is important. Even if this person does not immediately rejoin the discussion, he or she will be more likely to later on. If you fail to provide this kind of moral support from the chair, you risk losing the participation of the offended person for as long as you remain the chair.

Time to Adjourn

The time to adjourn any meeting of a committee or the board is when the agenda has been completed. If this principle seems self-evident, consider the meetings you have attended that were allowed to turn into bull sessions. Such impromptu, informal sessions can be very useful on occasion, but when you have completed your agenda adjourn the formal meeting. Then those who wish to remain for informal discussions may do so, and those who have commitments elsewhere can feel comfortable about leaving.

Meetings are where the action is. Meetings are therefore worth your best effort whether you are a committee member or a committee chair, a board member or a board president. Each of you has a role to play. If you play that role to the best of your ability, the output of your board—its decisions—will be the better for your having made the effort.

4 Board Composition and Leadership Development

Of all the activities in which your board of directors is engaged, probably none is more important than leadership development—the identification, recruitment, nomination, election, and development of present and future board members. Without capable people, the work of your board cannot be accomplished. What ultimately determines the quality of the organization and its work is *the quality of its board of directors*. With all due respect to the role of capable CEOs, the CEO and other staff cannot perform to their full potential without the support of an effective governing board of directors. It is also true that many of the problems that beset boards would disappear if the board member selection process were done properly.

Effective Boards Are Deliberately Assembled

The most effective boards are usually those that were deliberately assembled. If your organization is to be guaranteed a strong board, the board must involve all of its members in a deliberate, ongoing effort to identify potential new members throughout the year. The board should determine the various characteristics it requires to be included among its membership. Then the full board and senior staff should be continually on the lookout for people who match these specifications. In this search, your board should make use of a file card system, similar to the Board Candidate Recommendation Card exhibited in figure 2-1 to capture the names of prospects as they are identified.

Each board and senior staff member should have a supply of these cards. Then, whenever a potential board member comes to

Figure 2-1. Board Candidate Recommendation Card*

The following named person would be a useful addition to the board of directors.

NAME: _____ STREET: _____

CITY/STATE/ZIP: _____ PHONE: _____

BUSINESS: _____ STREET: _____

CITY/STATE/ZIP: _____ PHONE: _____

BUSINESS/PROFESSION: _____

PERSONAL CHARACTERISTICS AND/OR SKILLS OF INTEREST: _____

_____

_____

OTHER ACTIVE COMMUNITY INVOLVEMENT: _____

_____

WHAT BOARD ACTIVITIES WOULD INTEREST THIS PERSON: _____

_____

RECOMMENDED BY: _____ DATE: _____
                        (Your Name)

_____

*Adapted from *Leadership Development and the Nominating Process.* Swanson, 1990.

mind, that person should fill out the card (not telling the potential board member since it is not yet known when you might want to contact this person) and turn the card in to the organization's office where it can be filed 1) by name (alphabetically) and 2) in a second file of desired characteristics for the board. This can be done using a computer data base system as well. Just as with other important records, an additional "insurance" copy of this file, cards, or computer disks, should be maintained off the premises. At *every* meeting, board membership should be an agenda item for the board president to *verbally* and *forcefully* remind board members and senior staff members of their responsibility to turn in the names of possible future board members.

Who Should Sit on the Board

Let's begin with some personal characteristics of board members which can be considered universally desirable. O'Connell (1985) provides such a list. He suggests as most important, "the ability to start and end every analysis and evaluation with the standard of what is right." This he follows with fairness, toughness and sensitivity, reliability, controlled ambition, flexibility, and enthusiasm. To these I would add commitment to the purpose and mission of the organization as well as the time available to participate fully in board and committee meetings. General Norman Schwarzkopf once said, "A great deal of the capability of an army is its dedication to its cause." The same can be said of the capability of a governing board of directors.

As to categories of board members, you would look first for an appropriate cross section of the community served. You would likely want an appropriate age, sex, and ethnic mix. You might want people drawn from, or people with links to, the community power structure. Clients or client representatives are a consideration in several fields of service. Geographic distribution might be important to some.

Certain specific skills are frequently wanted; among these fund raising and financial expertise are the most typically sought after. The smaller the organization and the more the board approaches or becomes the workgroup model, the greater the possibility is that other skills may be needed, such as program, public relations, buildings and grounds expertise, and so forth.

In general, a healthy diversity among board members is desirable. It is a mistake when too many of the board members come from the same background and share the same basic interests. What comes to mind, for example, is a church-sponsored retirement center which requires a majority of the board to be ministers; or the board of a group home for the developmentally disabled, the majority of whose members must be parents of developmentally disabled persons; or a choral society board whose members bring nothing other than their love of music to the board table.

It can also be an error to attempt to focus upon the more prominent or affluent members of your community. Such people should be invited to serve on the board of directors only if they have the time and the willingness to participate fully in the work of the board. To have it otherwise is to set a poor example for the other board members and is actually dangerous for the board member who is just lending a name. Governing board members who do not attend meetings with reasonable regularity are negligent and this could have unfortunate consequences in a law suit.

In the final analysis, each organization must determine for itself the qualities it seeks to have represented on its board. Many boards have found it helpful to make a determination as to the combination of characteristics and skills which make an optimum board for *their* organization using a tool such as the Board Profile Grid shown in figure 2-2. This grid illustrates a few possibilities, and each organization should develop its own grid based upon its own individual needs.

The Work of the Nominating Committee

You may eventually serve on your board's nominating committee. Since, as discussed above, your entire board should be involved in the year-round identification of potential new board members, and since a nominating committee should not make decisions about the next year's board until it has some experience with the current board, it is usually best for this important committee to be appointed in the sixth month of the organizational year. The appointments should be made by the board president and approved by the board of directors. The committee should consist entirely of—or at least a majority of—board members. The president should not serve as a member of this committee.

The nominating committee's first source of information and advice about what characteristics need to be added to the board for the next few years is the current board president. The board president should present an evaluation of the incumbent board as well as suggest whatever characteristics are likely to be needed on the board in the future to the members of the nominating committee. The nominating committee is not bound by the president's recommendations, but its members should at least listen to the president, who has probably the best overall view of the whole board.

Your nominating committee is building a leadership team; therefore, it should take an organizational view of its task, first identifying the nominee for the next year's board president and then working downward. When the nominee for the presidency has been identified and has agreed to serve if elected, the strengths and weaknesses of the probable next board president are known. With these characteristics in mind, the nominating committee can identify nominees for the remaining offices and obtain their agreement to serve if elected.

While the CEO should not serve on the nominating committee or play a role in its process, it would be sensible for the chair of the nominating committee to quietly check with the CEO in order to be sure that there are no personality difficulties between the CEO and the proposed nominee for the presidency. This should in no way suggest, however, that the CEO has any veto power over the decisions of the nominating committee.

When the nominating committee has identified the remaining officer candidates, it should begin to identify candidates for the empty seats on the board. This is when the card file (or data base) of names—to which you and your peers on the board have been regularly contributing—as well as the Board Profile Grid will be especially useful. Attendance and participation of those board members whose terms have not yet concluded should be reviewed at this time also. Some boards provide an opportunity to resign to any board member whose attendance at board meetings has been marginal and whose committee participation has been minimal or nonexistent.

The Invitation Process

It is one thing for the nominating committee to select nominees for officers or board seats; it is quite another to *persuade* the chosen ones to serve. All such invitations to stand for election should be made in face-to-face meetings, unless distance makes this impossible. When a new president is to be nominated, the incumbent president can often be useful in the invitation process. A particularly effective strategy is for the nominating committee chair and the incumbent president to meet over lunch with the intended nominee and extend the invitation to stand for election. The incumbent president will normally know better than anyone else the responsibilities entailed and time required to serve effectively in the office and can therefore explain to the nominee what is involved.

When other new officers are to be nominated, the nominating committee chair, the incumbent president, and the nominee for president can all be useful. The participation of the presidential

Figure 2-2. Board Profile Grid*

	Term Expires	Term Expires	Term Expires	Notes:
EXPERTISE IN:				
Financial Management				
Fund Raising				
Program				
Planning				
Public Relations				
INFLUENCE WITHIN:				
Power Group				
Business/Financial				
Ethnic				
Media				
Government				
OTHER CONSIDERATIONS				

Other considerations might be age mix, sex mix, ethnic mix, related organization representation, knowledge of field of service, and so forth. Size your grid according to whatever skills and characteristics your board may require. The above grid is a basic example, not a recommendation.

Fill in the name of a board member who will be here next year *at the top of each column and make a check mark under each name wherever that person brings one or more of these needed skills or other characteristics.*

_____

*Adapted from *Leadership Development and the Nominating Process*, Swanson, 1990.

nominee can be particularly effective, because this person has agreed to the largest commitment and is in the position to say, "I would like *you* on my team."

When new board members are invited to stand for election, personal meetings are also best. This is particularly effective if such invitations to serve are made by the incumbent president or the nominee for the presidency together with the chair of the nominating committee. Invitations to serve can also be made by members of the nominating committee, incumbent officers, or incumbent board members. The choice, of course depends upon who will have the greatest chance of extending a successful invitation to serve.

When the invitation is made to a prospective board member, the reasons this particular person is being asked to serve should be made clear. "We want *you*, because . . ." will create an excellent impression of your board in the mind of the potential nominee. It is also most important that the responsibilities that go with membership on your board be clearly stated, so that the candidate will know exactly what a commitment to serve will entail.

The fact that there will be an election notwithstanding, the slate of officer and board nominees assembled by the nominating committee should consist of a single candidate for each office and each board seat. These should, of course, be the best qualified candidates the nominating committee can find. Should those who vote find reason to be displeased with one or more of the choices, there should be an alternative slate mechanism (discussed below) for them to resort to in order to nominate alternative candidates. State, national, and professional associations are exceptions to the above inasmuch as a number of members usually seek the major offices and the open seats on the board.

Announcement of the Slate

I recommend that the final and complete slate developed by the nominating committee should be made known to the electorate (those with the power to vote) in your organization forty-five days before your annual meeting, assuming elections take place at the annual meeting, as is the practice in most nonprofit organizations.

The announcement of the formal slate should be followed by a thirty-day period during which alternative names or slates may be submitted by the electorate. I would further recommend that the number of those persons nominating an alternative candidate or slate equal the number of members of the nominating committee in order for the alternative nomination(s) to be legitimate. At the end of this thirty-day period all nominations should be closed. Any alternative candidates or slates that have been legally nominated can then be announced, along with the official slate, in the invitation to the annual meeting. Members of the electorate now have a reasonable period of time in which to consider the alternatives.

It is probably necessary in state, national, or professional associations to permit nominations from the floor at the meeting where elections take place. However, this is a poor practice for most nonprofit organizations in that it fails to provide the voters with adequate time to contemplate the choices. In most private nonprofit organizations, alternative nominations are a rare event. However, the possibility must be provided for.

Finally, some organizations hold elections two months before the annual meeting at which the newly elected officers and board members take their seats. This sixty-day period between election and taking of office is used to organize the board for the coming year. However, this organization of the board can also be accomplished in the forty-five-day period called for in the above recommendation (see below).

Making Good Committee Appointments

Assume that you are the nominee for president and are now waiting out that forty-five-day period between the announcement of your nomination and the annual meeting at which elections shall take place. You can turn this waiting period to excellent advantage by using it to plan sound committee appointments. One of the advantages of this forty-five-day interval is that you now know who the players are going to be, assuming there is no alternative slate. Even if there is, you can still accomplish much of the work of making committee assignments during this period. If you use this time for this purpose, immediately after your election you will be able to call a brief meeting of the new board following adjournment of the annual meeting, announce your committee appointments, and obtain board approval of these appointments. (Do not forget to ask the outgoing president to provide proper notice of this special board meeting in the invitation to the annual meeting.) You would thereby have your board organized from your first day in office. Thus, while these forty-five days are passing, you can use the time to accomplish the following tasks:

- Review all the committee positions to be filled.

- Review the talents and weaknesses of all the available people—board members as well as other available committee volunteers.

- Determine the interest of board members and other appropriate and available volunteers in committee assignments, using a questionnaire for the purpose.

- Review the past committee assignments of all of the available people.

- Assess the performance (perhaps with the help of the incumbent president) of all of the available people in their past assignments. You should not automatically repeat the same assignments; variety of experience is vital to the growth of board members. Future presidents who have had a variety of committee experiences are usually better presidents.

- Select the chairs for all committees and secure their willingness to serve. But do *not* ask for volunteers at a board meeting. Your choices should be made deliberately and not left open to chance.

- Fill out each committee with members, considering the desires of each committee's chair to the extent possible. Since you are responsible to see that each committee receives its fair and appropriate share of the available talent, the final choice (subject to board approval) must be yours. In this process, be sure to involve every board member in at least one substantive committee assignment.

- After your election, present a complete list of proposed committee appointments to your full board for approval at a special board meeting called for this purpose immediately following the annual meeting.

Done in this fashion, the board will be organized from the very first day of the new organization year. For the new president to wait until after elections to get this work done would mean that the board organization would not be complete for one to two months into the new year.

The Orientation of New Board Members

Once elected, the new president has a special responsibility to ensure that all new additions to the board receive a full orientation. (See the beginning of part 1, The Board and the Nonprofit Organization, for a list of materials that should be provided to new board members immediately upon their election.) Before leaving the annual meeting the new president should meet with the newly elected board members, the treasurer or chief financial officer, the CEO, and the chairs of any key committees. This group should agree upon a date for a new board member orientation before the first official board meeting.

Appointed Boards

If your board is appointed by an outside authority rather than elected as described previously, you can still use the Board Candidate Recommendation Card system and the Board Profile Grid to help identify candidates for board membership. When a seat on the board must be filled, provide the appointing authority with three names of qualified persons and request that, if possible, the appointment be made from among these three candidates. Many appointing authorities, wanting to make the best possible appointments, will welcome such guidance. Even if a current appointing authority ignores your advice, keep up the practice. Appointing authorities change from time to time and a new person with the power to appoint may prove more receptive to your guidance.

It's Continuity That Counts

The most important aspect of the board leadership development cycle is that it is a *continuous* cycle that must never be allowed to stop. The board president is the key to this continuity of effort, beginning with *forceful, monthly, verbal reminders* to all board members of the importance of turning in names of potential board candidates so that as large an inventory of names as possible can be assembled from which to obtain future board (or committee) members. If your board is just beginning this identification process, be patient. It typically will take three to four years before the card file (or data base) contains enough names to be really useful. Persistence during these first years is absolutely essential if you are to succeed at this most important endeavor.

Saying Thank You

As board president, committee chair, or board member, you should be continually alert for opportunities to recognize—publicly if possible—the good efforts of other board members and volunteers. Few of your peers on the board, or among its committees, likely accepted their assignments in pursuit of public recognition. Nevertheless, it is a rare person who would object to being told that he or she did an outstanding job. Timely and appropriate praise is a major ingredient of the glue that holds any good organization together.

5 Board Organization

Sometimes it seems that human beings have a distinct preference for acting first rather than thinking about the best way of accomplishing a task. As the saying goes, "When all else fails, read the instructions." Too often, board members fail to pay attention to their "instructions"—that is, the bylaws that hold the organization together.

Bylaws, should be regarded first and foremost, as a set of specifications for the structure of your organization. Bylaws should be as brief as possible, given the structure to be specified. They should be clearly written, avoiding legalese. And they should exclude items better treated in policy statements (your CEO's job description, for example). Finally, your organization's bylaws should be *your* organization's bylaws, developed to implement *your* organization's statement of purpose, and not simply copied from the bylaws of a similar organization.

The following are several critical points that every organization's bylaws should address.

Organization Is . . .

For the purpose of this discussion, *organization is the setting up of relationships through which people can work together in order to accomplish a predetermined set of goals.* And as I noted in part 1 these predetermined goals are the mission-related goals derived from your mission and purpose statements.

Your Organization's Power Base

Every nonprofit organization has a power base—members, corporators, clients, or, most common, the board of directors itself. Formal power in a nonprofit organization is typically expressed by: 1) who elects the board of directors, and 2) who amends the bylaws. There are five typical patterns:

1. *Power is vested in members of the corporation, or corporators.* Corporators are intended to represent the community served. They come to the organization by a variety of routes: election by the existing corporators, appointment by the board of directors, automatic members by being elected to the board of directors or, in some cases, by being the spouse of a board member. The corporators elect the board of directors and, less frequently, they often amend the bylaws.

2. *Power is vested in members.* These members are comparable to corporators in the preceding example; however, these are dues-paying members who pay dues in the expectation of receiving some form of benefit or service. Members of a YMCA, for example, often have the power to elect the board of the YMCA and to amend the bylaws, and each such member has one vote during the period covered by the dues paid.

3. *Power is vested in the board of directors.* A board of directors that has the power to elect its own members is referred to as a self-perpetuating board. Such a board would also have the power to amend the bylaws.

4. *Power is vested in clients, or consumers of services.* This structure is a variant of members of the corporation described above. An example might be senior citizens in a county being declared to be, upon registration, members of the corporation of the county area agency on aging. As our consumer-oriented society grows, people will seek and be given more power over those organizations that provide them with services. Thus, I suspect that we will see more of this form of power placement in nonprofit organizations in the future. Client or consumer corporators have the same powers as corporators in the first example above.

5. *Power is vested in other organizations or communities whose members or citizens receive services from the agency.* Each such organization or community is typically empowered to *appoint* (see part 4) one or two members of the agency's board of directors. This is another way of placing power in the hands of those who receive services. In this situation, the bylaws would usually be amended by the board.

Each of these organizational options has its inherent strengths and weaknesses. The most common power structure among nonprofit organizations is the self-perpetuating board. However, generally speaking, my preferred method of placing power is to make use of members of the corporation. Thus, the board is specifically accountable to some higher authority that represents the community being served. Although some corporators have been known to meddle in areas that are properly the responsibility of the board of directors, I believe a greater danger exists when an irresponsible, self-perpetuating board cannot be influenced or, if need be, replaced by a higher authority.

In the final analysis, the community is usually the most important stakeholder in nonprofit organizations. The board of directors are trustees for the community's interest in a nonprofit organization. Properly handled, the use of members of the corporation—i.e., community representatives—can facilitate the organization's contacts with its community and most important stakeholder.

A large group of well-chosen corporators, deliberately assembled and regularly communicated with (through newsletters and such), besides representing the community can also function as a reservoir to tap when fund raising, as well as for future board or committee members. When corporators are specified to be only consumers of services (as in 4. above), the organization can run the risk of not being able to benefit fully from this and might be well advised to open its ranks to nonconsumer corporators.

Appointed boards have two serious potential liabilities. First, the appointing authorities frequently do not have any idea what characteristics are needed by the board at any given time. Second, board members who are appointed too often regard themselves first and foremost as representatives of the local constituency who appointed them. In taking this view, such board members forget that as board members their very first responsibility is to govern the organization to the benefit of *all* of those who are served by the organization and not just those from their own constituency. Appointed boards can often influence for the better the nature and caliber of the appointments that are made, however, by communicating the current needs of the board to the appointing authority (see part 4, Board Composition and Leadership Development).

Since most bylaw amendments affect the functioning of the board of directors, the power to amend the bylaws is usually best placed in the hands of the directors—with the exception of the power to alter the power structure—when power is vested in members or corporators. Communicating the rationale for a bylaw amendment to a large group of corporators or members can be time-consuming and expensive. If the members or corporators retain the right to elect the board, this is, in most cases, sufficient power.

How Big Should a Board Be?

Small can be beautiful but the ideal board size will differ for every organization, because the size of the board is dictated by what the board must do. Board size, in part, can be determined by the number of committees needed and the degree to which you can use nonboard members on board committees. Allowing nonboard members to serve on board committees will permit a smaller board. Small boards, whose committees report directly to the board and which do not make regular use of an executive committee, are usually preferable to larger boards because: 1) the quality of deliberation is better in a smaller board; 2) smaller boards are less costly to maintain; and 3) communications between board members and between the board and the CEO are usually better.

Functions of the Executive Committee

The purpose of an executive committee should be to have a standby committee which, in a bona fide emergency, can meet quickly to make a decision on behalf of the full board that simply cannot wait until the next board meeting, and there is no time to gather the full board. Decisions made by the executive committee carry all of the authority of the full board of directors.

Every board member should beware of the not uncommon problem of letting the executive committee become a de facto board of directors, meeting regularly and doing much of the work that ought to be done by the full board. This is a common characteristic of a board that has grown too large. When the executive committee is allowed to usurp the role of the full board, those board members who do not sit on the executive committee usually begin to feel like second class board members—even if they do not say so. Another reason this is bad practice is that the full board is still responsible—legally as well as morally—for *every* decision made by the executive committee. The board of directors may delegate its workload, but never its responsibility.

Limiting Terms of Office Without Losing Outstanding People

The practice of what is usually called board member rotation has gained widespread acceptance. The most common system of rotation is based upon a rule of thirds. The board is divided into three so-called classes with approximately one-third of the board in each. One class is elected each year for a term of three years. In this way the entire board is cycled every three years. At the end of the first three-year term, an individual board member is eligible—not guaranteed, *eligible*—for a second three-year term. After a second three-year term, the board member is then ineligible for reelection to the board for at least one full program year.

Such a system of rotation guarantees that a few seats will open up each year, providing the opportunity to bring new blood to the board. The one liability in this system is that, at times, it may be in the organization's best interest to keep a particularly outstanding peron active with the board to prevent premature loss of that person during the usually required one-year absence. There are two legitimate escape routes from this situation. One solution (which will be described below) is to elect officers separately—not from among an already elected board—and thereby allow a particularly talented person to return to the board by virtue of being an officer. Appointing such a person to a board committee is the other route.

One caveat. If a board member has not worked out well during his or her first term, do not out of a sense of kindness reelect this person to a second three-year term. As observed at the beginning of part 4, the quality of the board of directors is the ultimate determinant of the programs or services provided by your organization. The best interests of your clients or constituents are your first concern and their interests are best served by having the strongest board you can assemble.

How Many Officers?

Most boards manage quite well with a president, vice president, secretary, and treasurer. In smaller organizations following the workgroup style of board (discussed in part 1) the workload and/ or complexity of the job might require an assistant treasurer or an assistant secretary. More officers than these can rarely be justified.

A few words about vice presidents and treasurers are appropriate at this point. Too often vice presidents have nothing to do other than to stand in for an absent president. It is better when the president assigns the vice president some specific responsibilities which help to lighten the president's workload. I do not believe that these responsibilities ought to be specified in the bylaws, however. The first consideration in selecting a vice president is to bring strength wherever the president lacks it. Thus, it is better to leave the vice president's task assignments up to the president. In most nonprofit community service organizations it is not wise for the vice president to automatically succeed to the office of president because this system can identify a future president up to three years before that person assumes the office—a potentially dangerous practice. It is difficult enough to project the board's needs in its president one year in advance, let alone three years.

Bylaws typically charge the treasurer with much of the responsibility which in real life is carried out by staff. The larger the organization, the more common this becomes. My own feeling is that it is wrong to hold an officer liable for actions he or she does not in fact discharge. Unless your nonprofit laws require the office, it might be better to do away with the office and hold staff responsible for financial functions subject to board monitoring against those major organizational CEO and staff control policies which were discussed in part 1. A finance committee might assist the board in this function, particularly if there is an endowment.

In states where the law requires a treasurer and in organizations where finances are handled by staff, the CEO might be named treasurer, without a seat or vote on the board. In smaller workgroup-type boards, the treasurer's role is likely to be more important and in some cases major financial functions might be entirely removed from the CEO and responsibility for them assigned to the treasurer.

Officers are most commonly elected from among an already elected board. However, this presents a problem when the logical choice for your next president has but one year left in a second three-year term. You will only have this president for one year before he or she must leave the board for a year. Many boards approach election of officers in a different way. They elect their officers separately and then the officers take seats on the board *by virtue of their office*. In stating the composition of the board when officers are elected in this fashion, your bylaws might read as follows: "The board of directors shall consist of nine *directly elected* members together with the four officers who shall take their seats on the board by virtue of their offices and who shall be elected as provided for in Article VII" (Article VII being the article dealing with the officers). Thus, the total board numbers thirteen. In such a case, the same electorate that elects the board members elects the officers. When this is done, the election of the officers ought to precede the election of new board members since one or more of the officers being elected might be leaving behind an unexpired term on the directly elected portion of the board which will then have to be filled by a new board member to complete the unexpired term.

Some will worry that this practice might encourage the election of a president or other officer who has had no previous experience with the organization; however, this does not usually happen. Neither nominating committees nor electorates have tended to nominate or elect outsiders as presidents—unless their organizations would be better served by doing so.

Should Officers' Terms Be Limited?

Officer terms should also be limited. There is growing acceptance that one year is rarely long enough in most nonprofit community service organizations, and that three years as president is probably enough. Consider electing your organization's officers to one-year terms, with reelection to a second and third one-year term permissible—*provided that reelection is justified by good performance.* After one has served in a specific office for three one-year terms, one would no longer be eligible to serve again in that office. I further recommend that after a person has served as president for three one-year terms, he or she should no longer be eligible for *any* office.

It is usually a poor practice for a past board president to step down into a lesser office, and while it is very often useful to return the immediate past president to the directly elected board for a normal term, it is best not to require the practice as on some occasions it would not be justified. For similar reasons, it is usually best if the office of immediate past president were not mandated by the bylaws.

Specifying Meeting Dates and Times

Dates should be fixed in the bylaws for: the annual meeting, regular meetings of the board of directors, and any committees which must meet regularly. Typically the wording will be similar to, "The board of directors shall meet the third Tuesday of every month at 3:30 P.M." It is also a good idea to establish a calendar of events for the board and the organization for the full board year and distribute it to all board members at the beginning of the new year.

Attendance Requirements

Board service is a commitment and the clients, constituency, and community have a right to expect that the board will be strong and effective. This means that regular attendance is required of all who would accept a seat on your board. Assuming your board meets monthly I recommend that your bylaws specify that any member who is absent from three consecutive *regular* meetings for any reason should be considered to have resigned. The board, of course, could grant in advance a leave of absence in the event of illness or other important circumstances. But I would also recommend that the board allow only one such leave for a board member during any three-year term.

Immediately following any third consecutive absence, the secretary should automatically send out a form letter thanking the offending board member for past service and accept the offending board member's implicit resignation in accordance with the appropriate article and paragraph of the bylaws. I recommend that you go one step further and state in the bylaws that four absences from *regular* meetings for any reason during a program year also be considered a resignation. When absenteeism is handled in this fashion, the board is relieved of having to take overt action against one of its members—something that experience shows few boards are willing to do. This process is automatic and required under the bylaws, the requirements of which are well known to all.

Reasonable Quorum Levels

For boards of twenty-one or fewer members, 51 percent of the current membership should constitute a quorum for doing business at a regular or special board meeting. For those few boards which must be larger—typically state, national, and professional associations—and where long distance and weather might be a factor to consider, one-third of the board might be a more realistic quorum. For committees, 51 percent of the current membership is an appropriate quorum. For members of the corporation at meetings of the corporation, it is becoming more commonplace to see quorums set at whatever number of corporators appear for the meeting. You should check your state's nonprofit laws for any requirements as to quorums for meetings of members, however.

Should Bylaws Require an Annual Audit?

Absolutely! Your board should approve the appointment of an outside auditor, possibly recommended by your finance committee or your treasurer. If possible, the auditor should be a CPA or an accounting firm and the audit should be paid for. In addition to providing the board with an accurate accounting of the financial state of the organization, a good outside auditor can be helpful to staff in recommending good internal accounting practices. The audit should also review CEO compliance with the board's major organizational CEO and staff control policies in the budget and financial areas. As noted in part 1, an annual audit is an important element in the board's fundamental responsibility to monitor the management of the organization's funds.

Who Should Write the Bylaws?

As noted earlier, bylaws should be regarded as a set of specifications for the organization structure *you* have determined is necessary to achieve your purpose, mission, and mission-related goals. And whenever any of these is changed, the bylaws ought to be reviewed to assure that changes are not also necessary in the bylaws to be consistent with the revised purpose, mission, and/or goals. This means that the original author(s) of your bylaws should be people whose orientation is primarily organizational, not legal. Then, once the necessary structural determinations have been made, and before they are formally adopted, the bylaws should be reviewed by your legal counsel to be sure that they are legally correct—particularly with respect to your state's nonprofit laws and any legislation which may affect your field of service.

Amending the Bylaws

The rules concerning amendments to your bylaws should not be burdensome, nor should they permit impulsive, spur-of-the-moment changes. As recommended previously, the power to amend the bylaws should be vested in the board of directors—with the single exception of the right to change the power structure when the board is elected by corporators or by the members in a membership organization.

A simple, yet disciplined, method of amending the bylaws is to permit a proposed amendment to be made at any *regular* meeting of the board of directors. If the sense of that meeting is that the proposed amendment has merit and its language does not require additional time to draft, the proposed amendment should be announced to all board members within ten days of this first meeting, with the notice that the proposed amendment will be voted upon at the *next regular* board meeting. Thus a reasonable cooling-off period (assuming your board meets monthly) is built in to preclude hastily conceived amendments that might be regretted later. The patchwork quilt condition of many national association bylaws bears mute testimony to amendments presented from the floor, discussed, and voted upon all at the same meeting with little consideration given to the overall effect of the amendment.

As a normal procedure, any time your bylaws are amended, you should review the *entire* bylaws to be certain that the proposed amendment will not lead to unforeseen consequences. An ad hoc bylaw review committee should be appointed to conduct such an evaluation, preferably before the amendment is first presented, but, in any event, before the final vote is taken. Finally, any changes to your bylaws should be reviewed by your legal counsel.

Who Should Hire the CEO?

In the end, the final hiring decision must be made by the full board. However, the full board is usually too large to attend to all of the details in the hiring process. Your board must agree upon purpose, mission, and mission-related goals for the organization and it must have a clear idea of what it will expect of the new CEO. These expectations are the basis of the search.

A search committee is typically formed (not the executive committee) and should represent a cross section of the board. Some officers and key committee chairs usually are the principal members. Although the committee can be chaired by the board president, it probably should not be. As with all other committees, the president is a member ex officio. If the committee is not experienced in search procedures, it should get help. A personnel specialist, pro bono or paid, is probably the best choice to provide guidance.

Once the committee has reduced the candidates to, perhaps, three finalists, these should be interviewed by the full board in a structured situation where the same people ask the same questions in the same order of each of the candidates. The board then makes its decision.

Should the CEO Have a Contract?

Yes. I would recommend that for a new CEO, a one-year contract is advisable. However, upon satisfactory completion (based upon a performance evaluation as discussed in part 1) of that first year, a three-year contract will probably be appropriate. A succession of one-year contracts indicates a lack of confidence in the CEO on the part of the board. The contract should be fair to both parties and you should have the advice of counsel specifically knowledgeable in employee and labor relations when drafting it.

Should Close Relatives Serve in the Same Organization?

Generally speaking, no. While, to my knowledge, there is no law stating that husbands and wives should not serve on the same board at the same time, nonetheless, it is not a good idea. There is always the possibility of marital difficulties being brought into the boardroom. No close relative of the CEO or of any member of the staff should serve on the board because of the possibility and/or perception of conflict of interest. As for the staff itself, including the CEO, personnel policies often forbid close relatives being in the same supervisory chain, which would preclude them from serving in any except the largest of nonprofit organizations.

Afterword

In conclusion, it is important to mention that there are two *personal* gains to which every board member is entitled. The first is personal satisfaction from assuming this role and its responsibilities; the second is personal growth.

It is necessary that you, as a board member, take your responsibilities seriously, but there is no reason that you should not enjoy what you are doing. It is no accident that the most accomplished boards that I have been privileged to work with or to observe have been made up of people who take pleasure in and satisfaction from their work, and who enjoy working with the others in their organizations. Several years ago, one of the *Apollo* astronauts remarked, "A little levity is appropriate in a dangerous trade." A little levity is just as appropriate in the serious business of being a board member in a nonprofit community service organization.

The second gain to which all board members are entitled, and which they often achieve if they take their role seriously, is personal growth. Membership on the governing board of directors will frequently provide you with opportunities for experiences that you might not otherwise have obtained. For most of us, our lives will be enriched as a result; for some, such experiences can lead to major changes or advancement in their careers.

As in all of life's other opportunities, how effective you are, how successful your organization becomes, and how much growth and satisfaction you derive from your role as a board member will relate directly to the amount of effort you put into the job. My purpose in writing this book has been to try to provide you with the necessary knowledge and skills. The rest is up to you.

References

Cook, Jonathan. 1987. "Defining Purpose." *The NonProfit Times* November.

Carver, John. 1990. *Boards That Make a Difference.* San Francisco: Jossey-Bass, Inc.

Drucker, Peter F. 1974. *Management: Tasks, Responsibilities, Practices.* New York: Harper & Row.

Houle, Cyril O. 1989. *Governing Boards—Their Nature and Nurture.* San Francisco: Jossey-Bass, Inc.

Nason, John W. 1982. *The Nature of Trusteeship: The Role and Responsibilities of College and University Boards.* Washington, D.C.: Association of Governing Boards of Universities and Colleges.

O'Connell, Brian. 1985. *The Board Member's Book.* New York: The Foundation Center.

Swanson, Andrew. 1990. *The Collected Board Sense* (Issue D-64). Rumford, R.I.: Community Services Consultants.

———. 1992. *Evaluation—Bane? Or Boon?* Rumford, R.I.: Community Services Consultants.

———. 1990. *Leadership Development and the Nominating Process.* Rumford, R.I.: Community Services Consultants.